The 2 - Hour Vacation

Let Go and Relax
Reduce Stress & Anxiety,
Gain Inner Peace and Happiness

Original Edition

Sage Wilcox

The 2-Hour Vacation
Let Go and Relax, Reduce Stress & Anxiety, Gain Inner Peace, and Happiness

Copyright © 2016 Sage Wilcox

First Edition

All rights reserved. No part of this book may be reproduced, stored in a retrieval system or transmitted in any form or by any means, electronic, mechanical, photocopying, recording, or otherwise, without the written permission of the publisher.

ISBN-13: 978-1-945290-01-5

ISBN-10: 1-945290-01-3

Library of Congress Control Number: 2016906216

Printed in the United States of America.

DEDICATION

This is dedicated to all of the people who are working hard and doing their best while trying to better their situations day by day, in every way. Perseverance pays off. YOU deserve a break and this book is for you. Enjoy!

CONTENTS

	Acknowledgments...	i
	Preface..	v
	Section One	
1.	The Importance of Relaxation............................	1
2.	Leisure Through Learning.................................	9
3.	Create Some Leisure Time................................	17
4.	Physical Activity..	23
5.	Nature...	29
6.	Reconnecting with Family & Friends....................	35
7.	Unplugging...	41
8.	At Home Spa...	47
9.	Brighten Up Your Home...................................	53
10.	Be a "Tourist"	59
11.	Give Back...	65
12.	Vacation with Yourself.....................................	71
13.	Your Inner Child...	79
	Section Two..	87
1.	I Think Therefore I am.....................................	91
2.	How The Mind Works.....................................	97

3.	The Vacationing Mind............................	103
4.	You Can Do This at Home........................	107
5.	The Rhythm of Silence...........................	113
	Conclusion...	115
	Afterword..	117
	What We Do.......................................	119
	About the Author..................................	123

ACKNOWLEDGMENTS

This book is dedicated to all of the people who are working hard and doing their best while trying to better their situations day by day and in every way. Perseverance pays off. YOU deserve a break and this book is for you. Enjoy!

Deep, humble appreciation to the Divine Source, whom I aspire to grow closer to every day, with great faith.

Thanks to all who made this book possible. Also to those who loved and supported me as I worked on getting it published. You know who you are, and I am so appreciative and grateful. And last but not least, to the readers. Thank you for taking the time to read this book. I hope you enjoy it and find something inside that resonates and inspires you in some way. Thank you. Let's pour our favorite drink, find a comfortable spot, and get started, shall we?

"The purpose of a vacation is to have the time to rest. But many of us, even when we go on vacation, don't know how to rest. We may even come back more tired than before we left."
~ Nhat Hanh

PREFACE

I accidentally discovered the 2-hour vacation method one evening after I realized that my husband and I hadn't been on a "real" vacation in years. As a married couple of 15 years, with four children, we haven't had the luxury of going on a vacation in over ten years. And the few vacations we had prior to that were no more than 3 days at a time. For our own sanity and almost out of a survival instinct, we decided that we had to come up with a way to get more rest and relaxation in shorter amounts of time. We were stressed out and borderline depressed, although my husband says I *was* depressed. What, wanting to go to bed at 6 pm isn't normal? But how were we going to do this? It took time, practice, and dedication, but we think we figured it out and we know that we can't be the only ones looking for ways to bring peace, happiness, and contentment into our lives. The first thing we did, after some discussion, was ask ourselves what we would do within the next few hours if we were actually on a "real" vacation. And then we took action and actually did the things that came to mind. We discovered that 2-hour vacations are *real* vacations and we've been reaping the benefits, physically, spiritually, mentally, and emotionally, ever since. We've also been sharing this discovery with others who want the same. Come along, friend, relax with us for a while. You deserve it!

We all take vacations for various reasons, but almost none of them achieve the subconsciously desired result of being able to rejuvenate in a meaningful way. They are prefaced by the wrong notions and punctuated by false expectations. Most vacations are structured incorrectly from the start and usurp more vitality than imbue peace in the end. The typical vacationer returns home with great pictures, interesting souvenirs, and a hefty bill while what they really needed - what their soul really needed, was some time to still the madness.

Commercial advertising aside, our mind and body

demand down time for more than just the hope of getting out from under stressful and repetitive demands of our jobs. It doesn't matter if you are at a job you love, or at one that you hate, a job is a job, is a job. Then there are the everyday responsibilities that you have outside of your job. And they all tug at you. This adds up.

But believe it or not, stress is not about how much the job demands of us, it's how much we are able to stand up to the demands. We all have thresholds, and vacations are a way of reinforcing those thresholds and fortifying the spirit. With the right balance of vacation and work, there is nothing, absolutely nothing, that the human spirit cannot achieve.

Two things happen when the weekend approaches, though. The first is that you feel the bounce in your step - a little more energy, as you, otherwise, limp across to the finish line. And second, you see things in a better light, therefore, you respond to things more positively, and more often than not, people tend to finish out the week better than they started it on Monday morning.

But then the weekend comes and we unknowingly engage in all the wrong remedies for the weary week, prior. By Sunday night, although we may have had a load of fun, lots of socializing, events and merriment, we are worse off internally. We just don't know it yet because it's masked by the happy hormone, endorphin, from all the activities of the weekend.

Can you guess when the downside of all this shows up? That's right - it shows up bright and early Monday morning. National statistics rank Monday mornings as the most common time of the week for heart attacks. Also, statistically, more than one-third of all sick-leave days are taken on Monday. Two reasons for this: either people are so stressed out that the body just breaks, hence the heart attacks or they are so depressed that they fake the sick day. Either way you look at it, the evidence points to a toll on the psyche during the week that does not get fixed on the weekend.

Each time we take away from our soul during the week, and fail to replenish it adequately daily, or even weekly, it creates a net deficit in our body's ledger. Small deficits are offset by the reserves stored deep inside. And pretty soon, since there is no overdraft facility, we hit a wall.

In the United States, 42% of people don't go on vacations in a given year. That's almost half of the entire adult population who keep their stresses locked up. They continue being over-worked, over-tired with not enough rest and relaxation, and they cross their fingers that their reserves will cover the year's deficit.

The essence of a vacation is to allow the mind and body to recuperate from the wear and tear of the workplace. This wear is not just the cause of sore muscles, it is the source of mental, psychological and spiritual fatigue. It is the main cause of depression, it is the leading cause of psychosomatic illnesses, and in many cases, a depressed immune system.

A proper vacation does three things. It takes you away from the stresses and demands of your daily life; it gives your body time to heal and rejuvenate; and, it invigorates your mind by returning you to your natural rhythm.

But, we often confuse our body's call for a vacation with the idea of travel. Which is fine in most cases, but physical travel brings with it, its own set of stress and wear. If you want to experience the sights, sounds, and sensations of a tourist destination, that's fine on its own. But if you want to rejuvenate, and you should, then there is something more effective, more appropriate and better suited.

You don't have to go on expensive vacations, or even cheap ones. You can continue to be one of the 42% and stay home. We'll tell you how to get the same benefit as a great escape, all without leaving the comforts of your own home.

It doesn't matter if you are financially liquid and can afford luxurious jaunts, or not. It doesn't matter. Rejuvenating is for everyone and never about spending money. We all need it and we can all get it because the old adage that the best things in life are free is indeed true. It's a good thing that the best things in life are free because it's best to take these kinds of power vacations at least once a week, if not once or twice a day. If taking a power vacation once a week, or daily, seems impossible to you, don't worry. It's just a new way of thinking that we intend to help you explore.

The objective is to enjoy the effects of a vacation without actually going anywhere and the trick here involves a mind hack and we will walk you through it.

The first part of this book will give you ideas for mini vacations, and the second part will teach you the secret to actually relaxing your mind. With practice you will change the way you think and you will reap the benefits in every way possible. Enjoy your 2-hour vacations, friends. You deserve to live a vacation filled life full of peace, tranquility, and contentment.

The 2 - Hour Vacation

Let Go and Relax
Reduce Stress & Anxiety,
Gain Inner Peace and Happiness

Original Edition

Sage Wilcox

1
THE IMPORTANCE OF RELAXATION

Have you forgotten how to relax? Here in the United States most of us work too much without taking enough leisure time. This is unfortunate because taking time off improves our health, relationships, and our thinking. Additionally, studies indicate that when we do return to work, after our time off, we are more efficient and productive than we were before.

Even though vacationing is good for us, most people simply can't go away to an exotic land for a week or two. Hope is not lost, however; there is good news. You can reap the benefits of taking a vacation by escaping for an hour or two a day, or even every two days through "mini vacations."

The mini vacations that will be discussed in this book will help you achieve a *vacation mindset* through different activities. When you access this mindset regularly it becomes easier and easier to switch into this frame of mind.

In a nutshell, this book was written to remind you how to relax. It is broken into different categories of relaxation. It describes the benefits you will reap when you enjoy leisure time in all categories to keep you motivated. It also suggests activities you can do for each category. Finally, it provides you with tips on how to do these things in the best way possible.

You will learn that many of these categories touch upon each other and are closely intertwined. You will also learn how to relax and savor life, be a more enjoyable person to be around, and be more productive when you *are* working.

Are you taking enough time to relax? Chances are, you aren't. In fact, you are most likely overworked. It may startle you to hear that most of us are working longer hours now than ever before. Actually, here in the United States, we are working more than *any other* country in the industrialized world. But is that really so surprising?

It may not be surprising because we consistently report feeling overworked. Our economy isn't what it used to be and the rate of unemployment is high. As a result, those of us blessed to have jobs are feeling more pressure to clock in for more hours and take less time off. Additionally, many of us are working more and not receiving extra pay. In 2007, 24% of employees and 47% of employers reported that they invest an extra six or more hours a week at work without compensation.

Even our time off the clock involves work. 22% of those who are employed have reported that they feel obligated to respond to work emails at any time of the day. What's more, half of us check our email on the weekends. And *one-third of us* checks and respond to work emails while *we are on vacation*.

A rough economy, alone, isn't causing us to be overworked. Even in the 1990s when the economy was doing better, we were still working too much. Back then, we were working to what totals one month more per year than we did in 1970. In 1999, more than twenty-five million Americans regularly worked at least forty-nine hours a week. Eleven million of those people worked even more than fifty-nine hours a week. Although it is important that we be productive citizens and put in time at work, maybe we need to respect the importance of leisure time and relaxation a little more.

The Negative Effects of Too Much Work

There must be some benefits for all of our hard work, right? It's sensible to assume that all of these extra hours must be increasing our efficiency and our work productivity. However, 24% of people working excessively admit that working too much has caused a lot of mistakes on the job. Ironically, one in five Americans reported that they have *missed* work as a result of work-related stress.

Work performance isn't the only thing that is suffering. Excessive work is also affecting our families. As more stay-at-home mothers and fathers take part-time jobs to make ends meet, household chores that the stay-at-home parent would have normally completed go unfinished. What this means is that both parents are now working jobs and also working to do household chores – decreasing our overall time at home that was once devoted to leisure.

In addition to decreasing our productivity at work and causing a strain on familial relationships, chronic stress from lack of leisure time and excessive working results in more illnesses, increased injuries, and an overall decrease of general well-being. When we are chronically stressed, our levels of cortisol and epinephrine rise to dangerous levels. These "fight or flight" and stress-related hormones increase blood pressure, cause depression and anxiety, and put us at risk for heart disease.

IT IS TIME FOR A BREAK

It doesn't have to be like this.

- Men are 32% less likely to die from a heart attack when they vacation, women are 50% less likely.
- Women who take vacations say that they are happier with their marriages than those who do not.
- Even children are more likely to succeed academically with regular vacations.
- Taking time off regularly improves our quality of sleep and keeps us young. (Chronic stress accelerates the aging process.)
- Leisure time helps promote a healthy body weight as cortisol (a hormone that spikes with stress) increases belly fat and causes weight gain.

Even though we may not get to relax as much as we want to, we do realize that leisure time is precious. According to surveys, we value the memories and experiences gained from leisure more than any material goods that might be acquired through excessive work. We've all heard that familiar saying; "Those who are on their death beds never say they wished they would have worked more."

And we *want* to vacation. Seventy-four percent of Americans surveyed believe taking vacations is extremely important and eighty-eight percent of us realize that vacations are linked to rest and relaxation.

Although you may not have an opportunity right now to take time off and go away for a week or two, this book will teach and encourage you to indulge in "mini vacations." Getting an hour or two of leisure time once a day can help reverse the damages of overworking. With practice, you will become better at switching into the "vacation mindset." You will find it easier to unplug from your time at work and relax more efficiently. That's right, you can actually become more efficient at relaxing. And when you relax more, you actually become more productive at work – a win-win situation.

There are different ways to get into the relaxation mindset by taking "mini vacations." And I will give you tips on how to enjoy your leisure time more and give you ideas for activities you can do in each category discussed. The first way you can actively access relaxation is by learning new things.

"If your work requires you to travel, you will understand that there's no vacation destination like home."
~ Park Chan-wook

2
LEISURE THROUGH LEARNING

If you spend a "mini vacation" learning something new, your body and mind will thank you. The more education we have, the more skills we have in our tool belts, and the easier it is to solve problems and access what we need to help ourselves.

Learning something new that we are interested in helps us relax and take our mind off of things because we become engaged when we throw ourselves into the activity. This engagement leads to a feeling of fulfillment. When we are absorbed in this activity we lose track of time – although we might be tired after we spend an hour or two learning, we emerge from our activities happy and energized, a condition called "flow."

When our minds are challenged, our health and level of happiness are improved greatly. Not only is learning a great escape from our daily lives, it improves our physical and mental health. For example, doctors tell us that engaging our minds regularly can prevent Alzheimer's disease. Besides, learning something new doesn't have to be boring. Don't associate learning with high school math class: when your mind is busy learning something that you find fascinating it kicks into high gear.

Here are some ways you can reap the benefits of learning something new and exciting:

Learning Just for the Heck of It

What should you spend time learning about? How about learning something just for the sake of learning? Tackling a new mental challenge, that you have never really explored before, takes your mind off of day to day problems and improves your mental and physical health while you try.

Here are Some Things You May Never Have Learned About Before:

- → If you have never done so, spend an hour or two figuring out how to bake a loaf of bread from scratch – then enjoy the fruits of your labor for dinner.
- → Practice becoming proficient in handwriting with your non-dominant hand. The novelty will engage you and help you to lose yourself in the activity.
- → Learn about the unknown. Read up on four political leaders from countries you know little about.
- → Push yourself to explore the ideas of a religion you do not practice – it may result in a deeper understanding of your own beliefs and religion.

Learning with Purpose

As previously mentioned, the more you learn, the more skills you have in your tool belt. Spending a little time to learn with purpose can still feel novel and you will be more helpful to the people around you.

Helpful Things You Can Learn to do:

→ If you have never changed a diaper, spend time with a relative or friend who has children and learn how.
→ Take a course in CPR – The course will help you to engage your mind and relax, and it may very well come in handy one day.
→ Learn how to drive a stick shift. You could borrow a friend's car, or even rent a car for the day.
→ Sign up for a free course in self-defense – like a course in CPR, a course in self-defense will be engaging and may, in fact, come in handy one day as well.
→ Track the lineage of your family. You can go to the library to learn about your relatives, or sign up for an online service to help you.
→ Take an hour or two a day to learn a new type of code and use it on an app or website you have designed.
→ Figure out how to become a great public speaker *especially* if the idea of public speaking makes your cringe.
→ Learn how to upcycle, that is re-purpose old items from your house and sell them or give them as gifts.

During the course of your self-education, you will become more effective at learning. Start by embracing your *learning style*.

Learning how to Learn

Most people acquire knowledge best through a sensory experience involving touch, hearing or sight. It is possible to learn more efficiently by focusing your learning efforts on one of these senses.

-Are you a hands-on learner?

1. If you learn best through incorporating physical activity and the sense of touch into your endeavors, try to learn new ideas by touching, building models, and moving

around while you consume new content.

2. Although this may sound outlandish, you may be able to memorize and understand ideas better by performing small skits, or talking through them while you pace back and forth.

-Are you a visual learner?

1. Write down information that is important to you in a way that you will remember and understand it best – use post-it notes and highlighters to color code important concepts, ideas, and instructions.

2. Easily remember important pieces of information by using flash cards, or drawing pictures that will explain new ideas you would like to remember

3. Spend extra time looking over graphics and visuals, and draw pictures to help you understand new ideas better.

-Are you an auditory learner?

1. As you process important information that you would like to retain, read directions or content out loud as you go through it.

Find things that you enjoy. How do you know if you enjoy something? It feels good when you do it? Time also goes by very quickly when we are doing things that we enjoy. Gardening might not be good for one person, but it might be extremely relaxing and rewarding for another. Start to listen to your inner being. Let it guide you. When something feels good, that is your internal compass telling you something. Keep moving in that direction. Continue to try new things. Vacations are often times exciting because we try new things and visit new places. Life can be a vacation, friend. Life can be an adventure more than just once or twice a year. Learn new things with a vacation mindset

THE 2 – HOUR VACATION

Remember vacation is a mindset. If you were on vacation right now, what would you be doing? Do those things in shorter time spans and enjoy!

*"For me, the best vacation is just
relaxing on the couch!"
~ Scotty McCreery*

3
CREATE SOME LEISURE TIME

Taking a mini vacation to explore and to increase the amount of creativity you have in your life will reduce stress, improve any negative emotions you may have such as depression, and can help you to control anxiety. When you tap into your creativity, you are expressing yourself in a meaningful way that you can share with the world or enjoy on your own.

Imagination, the act of shutting down the logical part of your brain, can harness your creativity and it will cause you to be more open-minded, boost your self-esteem, and allow you to change perspectives with ease.

Interested in being more creative but don't know where to start? Here are some ideas to get your creative juices flowing:

- ✓ Pick up a simple instrument that is easy to learn and write your own tune. A recorder, simple harmonica, even a tambourine is amazingly fun to play, easy to master, and will give you a better ear for music.

- ✓ Get a book on origami and start folding. You might be surprised at how stimulating and engaging an hour or two of origami can be.

- ✓ Paint. There are endless possibilities for subjects, and a variety of mediums you can use to paint.

Activities You Can Do

- Enjoy some creative writing. Don't worry about how good your story is, just write what strikes your fancy! If you are suffering from a serious case of writer's block, write down every idea that comes to mind – literally. Even if you are just writing about how you cannot come up with a thing to write about, you are still tapping into your creativity and becoming an author!

- Draw portraits without making any effort to learn how to draw. Simply observe a friend, family member or stranger and try to translate what you see onto paper. Draw a flower, or tree. Draw whatever catches your eye. Spending time to do this is calming and will change the way you perceive the things around you.

- Make up some great jokes, or even work on a stand-up routine. You don't have to do a routine on stage if you don't want to, but there are few things more enjoyable than a good laugh, or making those around you laugh too.

Some Tips to Use in Your Efforts

Realize that creativity is a numbers game. Do not allow yourself to feel frustrated if you feel like the art, music or ideas you are producing are "no good." Remember even the most famous artists or prestigious writers have produced thousands of works that were considered to be no good – only a handful of their creations have become "masterpieces."

Surround yourself with vivid colors to enhance creative thought. Blue is considered to be a creativity-inducing hue.

Before you tap into your creativity, do "warm-ups." For example, come up with fifty completely new uses for a simple fork. If you are having difficulty turning off the logic in your brain, close your eyes and draw doodles on a notepad.

Try to write short stories from a perspective that is entirely unfamiliar to you – such as the point of view of a four-year-old or even a cat or dog.

Take old pieces of paper and bundle them into small notepads. Place a notepad on your night table, one in the kitchen and one in front of the television and capture any inventive idea that comes to mind.

Begin a dream journal – some of the most creative times of our lives are experienced during sleep.

Finally, if you are feeling frustrated by any constraints to your creativity, embrace them completely. Dr. Seuss wrote the famous book "Green Eggs and Ham" on a bet that he could write a book using fifty words or less.

Remember vacation is a mindset. If you were on vacation right now, what would you be doing?

"I'm a very anti-vacation person. Because I'm always getting on planes for work, to me, a vacation is when I don't have to get on a plane."
~ Gilbert Gottfried

4
PHYSICAL ACTIVITY AS A MINI VACATION

Physical activity is a great way to relax, and we all know the mental and physical benefits of regular exercise. While running miles, doing circuits or lifting weights is absolutely beneficial, if you are not already experienced with and accustomed to these activities, they may feel like a chore to you at first until you become used to the exercise.

However, taking an hour or two to be physically active on a regular basis, even if you are less experienced doesn't have to be painful. It can be enjoyable, stimulating, fun and relaxing. Getting active reduces the levels of cortisol and epinephrine in our bodies, the hormones associated with stress, improving health and easing symptoms of stress. When we are tense, physical activity is a great way to release negative energy, or if we are sluggish from too much work, it is a way to get energized and prepare for the next work day.

Here are some activities that people who do not regularly exercise might enjoy. The key to using activity to relax is to not associate exercise with body image or losing weight. Your main priority should be to enjoy yourself with a free hour or two that you have set aside for leisure.

-Buy a trampoline from a discount store or yard sale and start jumping.

-Go for a bike ride through your neighborhood or the park.

-Play Frisbee with some friends or your dog in the backyard.

-Get a group of friends and play a round of dodge ball.

-Go to the playground at night and get in touch with your inner child.

-Learn how to ride a horse and enjoy a ride on a nice day.

-Enjoy some sports, like soccer, rugby or field hockey.

-Sign up for a charity walk, you can socialize, get some exercise, and benefit a great cause at the same time.

-Jump rope for as long as you can. Although this may seem like a lightweight activity, it is actually quite vigorous – boxers jump rope to stay in peak condition.

-Get a video game that encourages physical activity. The "Wii Fit" is an example of an older gaming system that gets you up and moving while having fun.

-Dancing isn't just a thing to do at a party – it is a high energy aerobic workout that is a lot of fun to do on your own, too. Turn up the volume and start dancing.

-Volunteer for a cause that will have you do manual labor, like Habitat for Humanity. If you cannot dedicate yourself to such an activity, sweep an older neighbor's driveway, or rake leaves for a friend who is too busy.

-Find a new trail – in a park, the forest, or even an area of your neighborhood or city you are not familiar with and begin to explore it.

-Hula hoop. You might discover that after a while of doing it, your abs have gotten quite the workout!

-If you are around a pool, the beach or a body of water, play in it. Doing laps might not be great for beginners, but even doing the doggy paddle for an hour can be a great workout.

Activities You Can do with the Family

You can bond with your family and enjoy the relaxing benefits of exercise at the same time. Physical activity is a great mini vacation to enjoy with your family members.

-Have a dance party with the children. Shut off the lights, play some 70's disco music and use a flashlight as a strobe.

-Work in the yard with your kids rather than having them do the chores by themselves. Teach them how to grow healthy foods that they can pick themselves.

-Take the dog for a long walk with the family. Your pet is a member of the family too!

-Have a sport's night. Sports don't have to be incredibly intense, they can be hopscotch or twister.

Switch Things Up to Keep the Ball Rolling

To ensure that you stay motivated and continue getting exercise, vary what you do. Vary the type of activity you engage in, vary the room or place where you exercise, and although exercising right before bed may prevent good sleep, switching the times at which you exercise can decrease procrastination because you are not anticipating the activity.

Tips to Stay in Shape for Your Physical Activity

You will want to be sure you are in good enough shape to partake in regular activity. Park far away from the stores you frequent and the office you work at and walk. Take the stairs in lieu of the elevator. If you really want to go for the gold, hold yourself accountable by leaving a post on Facebook declaring that you are going to start exercising more. Make great playlists – dance music, funk, and hip-hop are great tracks to exercise to. If you are trying to improve at an activity, focus on your form, and maintaining a good stature for the exercise rather than the temporary physical discomfort you might experience. However, listen to what your body is telling you. If you overexert yourself, you will be tired and sore the next day when you are trying to work. Remember enjoying activity in order to relax should be about leisure, not about pain before gain.

THE 2 – HOUR VACATION

"To take a job just so I can go on a fancy vacation doesn't really seem worth it."
~ Melanie Lynskey

5
ENJOYING NATURE ON YOUR MINI VACATION

According to the Center for Disease Control and Prevention, people from areas like Hawaii, Florida, Arizona and Los Angeles are happier, overall, than people who live in colder climates. This is because spending time outside is good for your mental health, and physical health as well.

Take Vitamin D, for example. This vitamin is beneficial and necessary for your health. Too many office dwellers suffer from a Vitamin D deficiency due to a lack of natural sunshine, which can take a toll on the body's health.

Sunshine is also good for the body's internal clock – it keeps us balanced during the day and ensures that we get a good night's sleep. Finally, when you are outside, you are naturally more active, and activity, as discussed above, is a great way to relax as well.

Here are some things you might enjoy doing to tune into nature more in your life:

-Go flower picking, and give a bouquet to a good friend or neighbor to brighten their day.

-Get a book on bugs, walk through the backyard, and learn about these little creatures as you take a stroll on a sunny day.

   -While you're at it, make sure you are nice to all of earth's creatures. Flip a beetle over that is stuck on his back, or trap a spider under a glass and usher the little guy outside. It will feel a lot better than killing him.

-Learn about trees and snap some beautiful pictures at a local arboretum.

-Bring some stale bread to the pond and feed the ducks – these guys are always in for a snack!

-Take time to set up a bird feeder and fill it with seed. Although it doesn't take much time to fill a feeder with seed every day, drinking a cup of coffee in the morning while these beautiful creatures flock to it is exhilarating.

-During the night, look up at the sky and stargaze

-Make a contract with yourself: if you ever see a rainbow, immediately pull over to enjoy it, unless you are in a dire emergency!

-Invest money in a hammock and take a nap in the sun. It will be the best money you ever spent.

Respect and Appreciate the Environment

A rewarding and relaxing way to enjoy the beauty of nature is to develop respect for the environment. We owe a lot to nature – one study led by the Chiba University in Japan took two hundred and eighty participants, divided them into two groups, and placed half in the city, and the other half in the woods. The next day, they switched the groups and placed the city group in the forest and the forest group in the city. The researchers concluded that after spending a day in the forest, participants had lower cortisol, pulse rate, and blood pressure.

Being around plants actually makes your body healthier. The chemicals emitted by plants are called phytoncides. These increase the number of white blood cells in our body called Natural Kill Cells. These cells actually hunt down and kill infected body cells.

Spend More Time in Nature

When we are indoors, we are presented with an influx of distractions like televisions, computers, and of course, smartphones. However, being a little bored is a good thing. In fact, boredom increases creativity, which is another method of relaxation that has been discussed.

A great start to spend more time in nature is to simply do more activities outside -

Eat outdoors – have a nice cup of coffee on a cold winter morning to wake up, have a picnic on a fall day, or a barbecue on a summer night.

Exercise outdoors – Exercise is a great way to find relaxation, and you can double your stress relief efforts by enjoying exercise outdoors.

Socialize outdoors – When you host a gathering, rather than having drinks in front of the television, have drinks outside on the deck.

Partake in outdoor activities – Start a garden in the spring, set up an obstacle course in the fall, have a snowball fight during the winter, and take a stroll in the summer.

Finally, do yourself a favor and remind yourself every time you step outdoors to appreciate the weather of the day, even if it is dreary, cold and rainy. Force yourself to appreciate something about the day. Far too many people complain about the weather when it is completely out of their control.

Remember vacation is a mindset. If you were on vacation right now, what would you be doing?

"To me, 'Vacation' means titillating my taste buds."
~ Brett Ratner

6
TAKE A MINI VACATION BY RECONNECTING WITH FRIENDS AND FAMILY

Healthy relationships are the bread and butter of happiness and life satisfaction. When we are around other people we care about, it is an opportunity to place others ahead of ourselves. Not only do relationships with partners, friends, children and family present us with fun and fulfillment, you also get to enjoy the social support and the expertise of your favorite people.

Enjoying time with the people we like best reduces stress and also bolsters health as well. One study conducted by Holt-Lunstad concluded that lack of social relationships can be equivalent to smoking up to fifteen cigarettes a day! Indeed, people who have strong social ties to the people around them live longer, and there is the fascinating "Michelangelo Phenomenon." When a partner sees you more like the person you want to be, it helps you actually become this person.

How to Reconnect

-The simplest way to begin reconnecting with your friends and family is to sit down and make a phone call. If you are worried about time constraints, just be open and honest, and tell the person you would like to connect with that you have an allotted time. Be sure to respect their time as well.

-The Internet can be overwhelming or an unnecessary presence in your life sometimes, but it also presents a great opportunity to find close friends or family members who you have lost touch with.

-Pets are friends and family members too. Being affectionate with animals can be good for your mental health, and everyone can benefit from sharing physical contact.

Spending an hour or two speaking to your close friends or family members, that you may have lost touch with, can be very relaxing and put you in the vacation mindset where it takes you away from your regular daily activities.

A Tip for Reconnection:

Now might also be a good time to take inventory of the people you speak to. Making peace with people you have had a falling out with will significantly cut down on negative emotions. Forgiving someone you are angry or unhappy with really benefits you the most, and letting go of grudges is a great way to improve your life. However, there may be some people in your life who are not so good for you and losing touch with them, without burning bridges, can be a good idea in some cases, as well.

Mini Vacations to Consider to Help You Reconnect with People You Care For

This book is full of ideas on ways to relax and enjoy a mini vacation. Relaxing with another person is a great way to bond even more. Spend time learning something together, sharing time doing creative things or volunteering together are all good ways to spend your time.

Some Relationships that Anyone Might Benefit from:

- Childhood friends that you met in grade school
- New acquaintances that may potentially be a good friend
- Companions to exercise with. You can find jogging groups, for example on the site Meetup.com
- Get to know someone who is younger than you to offer you a different perspective
- If you are not already close with your parents and siblings, now may be the time to get closer to your family.
- Join groups through your church. Church groups are a wonderful way to connect with like-minded people.
- Finally, make sure you are friendly with yourself. Being introspective, reflecting on your personality or constructively improving something about yourself will help you in your relationships with other people.

"My whole life is a vacation."
~ Leon Bridges

7
UNPLUGGING ON YOUR MINI VACATION

Some recent studies suggest that we are addicted to using our devices. Ask yourself: when was the last time you spent an entire day without glancing at your phone, surfing the Internet or skipped watching television in lieu of seeking a non-technology related way to spend your time?

Eighty-four percent of participants in studies have reported that they could not go a day without using their cellphones. Sixty-four percent of cell phone users check their phone for phone calls, texts or alerts even when they haven't heard any vibration or sound to let them know that they should. This indicates that too many of us use our phones excessively, to the point where it could be considered an addiction. In fact, we check our devices every six and a half minutes on average.

Compounding this problem, eighty-eight percent of consumers in the USA are using their cellphones *as a second screen,* using cell phones while watching TV or while we are on a computer. Our cell phone habits even interfere with our sleep schedule – almost half of the people who use cellphones have slept with their devices on so that they did not miss any type of alert or interaction. Finally, on average, we spend over six full days' worth of time distracted by technology for each month of our lives.

Unplugging for Even an Hour can be a Great Mini Vacation

You may be wondering why unplugging is a good thing, and why putting down your devices can improve your mental health, intellect and reduce stress. Ironically, using too much social media can damage our real-life social relationships. Research indicates that you can reduce unhealthy feelings like jealousy and loneliness by taking time off of social media. One in three people surveyed reported that they actually felt worse about themselves and dissatisfied with their lives after using Facebook. On a colloquial level, this makes sense. Consuming too much social media can make us feel bad about our bodies and lonely if our Facebook friends do not respond to our posts as much as we would like them to.

What's more, using media too much prevents you from exploring new ideas. For example, take Netflix. The algorithms that drive the program suggest things to watch that are similar to what you have already watched. The same goes for music and reading programs. Dissociating ourselves from these distractions leads to exploration.

If you think about it, devices and media can prevent you from finding contentment. The Internet, cellphones and social media produce a constant stream of notifications and alerts that will eventually create a fear of missing out that pervades life. This fear of missing out produces stress and negative emotions.

Finally, these distractions are essentially a big feedback loop. Consider this idea: if your friend gets bored at a store and starts browsing through their cell phone, this will cause you to look at your cellphone as well. Devices and their usage are like yawns: they are very contagious.

Unplug to Relax

Technology has made all of us terrified of boredom. But feeling boredom after putting down devices is not a sign that you need a distraction. It is a sign that you have become addicted to screens and media. Also, being bored is not a bad thing – feeling bored makes us use our imagination and encourages creativity.

Consider risking an hour of boredom as a way to take a mini-vacation. Spending your time doing something else is a great way to relax and improve yourself. Here are some ideas to help you easily put down the devices and stop staring at your screen.

-*Start the Day Off Right* – The beginning of our days sets the stage for the rest of the day. Spend the first hour of your day avoiding media distractions. Use this hour to meditate or plan the upcoming day.

-*Make Sure that You Unplug Regularly* – Try to spend forty days a year to power down unnecessary applications. Forty days is a small fraction out of a year comprised of three hundred and sixty-five.

-*Keep a Media Diary* – People who want to lose weight often begin their diets with a "food journal." Recording what they are eating makes people realize how much they are actually eating and the quality of the food that they are consuming. This sparks a desire to change. Try this with the media you use every day. Log when and what you are looking at. Chances are you are spending more time staring at a screen than you realize, and you will most likely find that the quality of the media you consume is poor.

- *Consume Better Media* – If after you have recorded what you are watching and doing for the day and you aren't happy with what you see; you can plan to spend an allotted time using technology in a healthier way. Watch a documentary instead of reality TV. Create media rather than just consuming it by creating your own YouTube videos or starting your own blog.

-Plan Ahead – It is a good idea to schedule watching television shows. You can record your favorite programs and watch them only while you are working out, or maybe on Sunday night to unwind before the work week.

-Prepare Others – A lot of the time we feel obligated to answer phonecalls or emails immediately. Prepare others by letting them know that you won't always have your phone turned on. Who knows, you may set an example for others to follow.

- Start Small – If avoiding media seems overwhelming, start small. When you go out to run errands, make a point to leave your cellphone at home or in your glove compartment. Move devices to a different room an hour before bed. Shut down your phone at the same time every night and don't turn it back on until the morning. Try to put down one gadget at a time to work up to a media detox – stop watching television first, avoid your computer second and stop using your cellphone for an hour or two a day so you can become accustomed to putting down devices using small steps.

The ideas that are discussed in this book that can be mini vacations are also excellent ways to spend your time more productively. Take advantage of the possibility you may have to relax by avoiding media and doing things that will help you turn your brain off and relax at the same time.

Remember vacation is a mindset. If you were on vacation right now, what would you be doing?

"Chilling out on the bed in your hotel room watching television, while wearing your own pajamas, is sometimes the best part of a vacation."
~ Laura Marano

8
TAKE A MINI VACATION BY CREATING AN AT HOME SPA EXPERIENCE

Pampering yourself with at home spa activities is a great way to take a mini-vacation for both men and women. Taking care of our bodies encourages feelings of contentment and improve our physical and mental health.

Soaking in warm water or cleansing your skin with hot water puts pressure on your body, making your heart work harder and keeps you healthier. Cleaning your body with a soak or a face mask will open your pores, which is a good way to get rid of toxins and deep cleanse your skin. Finally, when we feel good about ourselves we think better thoughts. These thoughts improve self-esteem and make you more confident.

Things You Can Do to Create an at Home Spa

There are a number of things you can do to pamper yourself for an hour or two. When you are preparing to engage in spa activities, be sure to unplug as was discussed above. Turn off your cell phone and ensure that there won't be any interruptions. Put on your favorite music and light some incense. Dim the lights to increase feelings of relaxation and enjoy a cup of tea or your favorite wine while you are doing these activities:

-Take a hot bath. If you would like, you can add milk and oatmeal to your bath water. This will moisturize your skin, leaving it smoother and softer. Try Epsom salts to relieve sore muscles, or add peroxide for a cleansing effect.

-Make a body mask with cosmetic clay and water. Rub this on your torso, legs and arms. Let this mask dry while you are drawing your bath.

-Give your muscles a massage. You can massage yourself, concentrating on sore muscles. It's good to be kind to your body!

-Exfoliate your body with a scrub or a loofah. This opens your pores and lets you detox and clean your skin better.

-After your bath apply body lotion on yourself and face moisturizers. Rubbing the lotion onto your skin will relax you, and you will feel better about yourself. This goes for both men and women.

-Give your face a steam by warming a bowl of water on the stove or in the microwave. Then, drape a towel over the back of your head, and lean over the bowl of hot water, cleaning your face and relaxing you.

-Clean your nails and shape them. Start by soaking your hand in a bowl of warm water for five minutes. This will soften your nails and your cuticles, allowing you to push the cuticles back, which will make your nails look better. Trim and file your nails to shape them.

You don't have to spend a lot of money to get a spa treatment or dedicate an entire day to do these activities. It is possible to set aside an hour or two every week to feel relaxed, improve your appearance and boost your self-esteem. It may surprise you to realize how invigorating a spa mini-vacation may be.

"My idea of a vacation is staying home and doing short day hikes, floating the river and things like that."
~ Tim Cahill

9
SPEND A MINI VACATION BRIGHTENING UP YOUR HOME

Cleaning your living space doesn't only make it nicer to spend time in, there are many health benefits to a clean, bright home. Chores may not seem like a relaxing activity but putting effort into completing them helps you to appreciate the more mundane activities in life. The work you do when you clean is repetitive, allowing you to throw yourself into the tasks, shut your mind off and go into vacation mode. There are also a lot of benefits to regular cleaning.

-Cleaning your home regularly helps you to cut down on allergens and dust. Sweeping, vacuuming, and dusting help rid the home of dust mites, pet dander, and dust which can cause people to have flu-like symptoms.

-Cleaning is a good workout. For every hour of chores, you do, you burn two hundred calories. Chores that burn the most calories include sweeping and mopping, mowing the lawn and scrubbing down surfaces.

-The cleaning process reduces stress and anxiety, according to the British Journal of Sports Medicine. According to this publication, twenty minutes of cleaning can improve your anxiety and stress by twenty percent.

-Cleaning your home increases your productivity. A messy, cluttered house is a serious distraction. Having a house that isn't overflowing with laundry, and things you don't need, helps you to focus more on the present moment at hand which will help you be more productive.

In addition to cleaning your house for an hour or two, you can do some easy and cheap redecorating that you will find stress relieving and it can improve the appearance of your living space. Redecorating is also just a really fun way to enjoy your time. Here are some ideas you can consider:

-Pick up cheap picture frames at the dollar store. Print out your favorite pictures or quotes and arrange the picture frames to complement the look of your house. You can get some cheap paint as well and paint the frames if you desire.

-Repurpose furniture to multitask. Consider picking up modular units (small storage boxes) for around twenty dollars and stack them on top of each other to use as nice looking accents and to organize your things better.

-Hang decorative plates on walls, making an arrangement. Mount colorful plates on your wall to fill empty space and to improve the appearance of your home. Plates are an original way to decorate and they are also inexpensive if you pick them up second hand.

-Wicker furniture is cheap and it is a great way to change the feel of any room. Rearranging your furniture and adding new pieces is a great way to alter the appearance of your living area drastically.

-For a rustic and relaxed look, hang natural objects, that

you have found at the beach, on the walls. Create a display or accent your shelves with seashells, sea glass, or rocks.

-Hang up mirrors to make your living space look larger and to add a touch of class to your home. Mirrors also add light to a room, brightening it up.

-Rather than placing books on a bookshelf, arrange a few in a pile. Carefully arranged books in a pile draw the eye in, attracting attention and adding to the look of the room.

By redecorating your living space and taking the time to clean it, an hour or two every week or so is a great way to engage in repetitive actions (like folding laundry) that will help you to relax and turn your brain off which will add satisfaction to your living area. As you have read, you can alter the appearance of your home dramatically with some inexpensive easy tweaks. You don't need a professional interior designer, hours of free time, or a ton of money to create a look for your home that you really love.

"Honestly if I get a vacation I'm gonna go and sit on my couch in New York."
~ Matt Damon

10
TAKE A MINI VACATION BY BEING A "TOURIST" IN YOUR OWN TOWN

This may seem like an odd thing to do, but being a tourist in your own town helps you appreciate the area you live in and see it from a different perspective. It is a way to escape because it adds whimsy to your life and can make you feel like you are away on vacation. However, it only takes an hour or two, so you can enjoy the feeling of avacation without spending a lot of money or having to take a lot of time off from work. You can "go on vacation" in the town you live in alone or as a family activity.

How to be a Tourist in Your Own Town

-Look for restaurants that offer a type of cuisine that you have never tried before. You can save money by joining a mailing list like Groupon, and wait for a coupon for restaurants that are new to you. This will give you the feeling of a vacation. First, you won't have to cook and second, you will be trying something you have never had before.

-Consider taking a tour of your town. If there are no tours available because you live in a smaller city, contact your town office. Or in larger cities, take the bus or the train that takes a different route than you are used to. Also, being able to observe your city from the perspective of a tourist will allow you to see your hometown in a whole new light.

-Take fun pictures of your town and at touristy areas in your town. Taking pictures of the area that you live in can be an interesting way to view your town from a different perspective while taking pictures of touristy areas in your town is just a fun idea and a way to capture memories with family and friends.

-Watch a local game, like your city's baseball team, or even a high school football game.

-Go to a bar where tourists and residents go. You can talk to new people from different places which is always a fun way to learn more about different cultures and your own culture at the same time.

-Head to an area of an attraction that focuses on the history of your hometown. If you need any ideas for things to do, head to a local hotel and pick up some pamphlets that suggest places to visit in your town. You can check your town's official website for ideas as well.

-Research things to do by reading local blogs and the local newspaper.

-To really see things from a different perspective, check review sites and websites like yelp to see what real visitors are doing in your town. Then, visit the places most tourists have seen. You can write a review yourself if you'd like which will help local businesses.

-If you really want the tourist experience, check into a local hotel.

-Use websites like meetup.com to immerse yourself into a group with people you don't know that is geared towards bringing visitors together.

-Invite a friend or family member to your area then spend a few hours showing them around town. Showing a loved one the areas you think are most interesting and special is a fantastic way to appreciate the beauty of your locale. These are just a few ways to be a tourist in your own town. If you brainstorm, you can surely think of additional things to do in your area as well. For some people, this activity may seem strange, but what could be more invigorating than learning to appreciate what is around you more?

Remember vacation is often exciting because of new people, places, and things that we experience. Many of us haven't even seen all that our very own home state or town offers. Vacation is a mindset.

"If some people didn't tell you, you'd never know they'd been away on a vacation."
~ Kin Hubbard

11
SPEND A MINI VACATION GIVING BACK

Volunteering your services to your community is a way to escape from your day to day responsibilities and feel better about yourself. Also, you are giving back to your community which is also a great reason to volunteer your services.

There are many benefits to doing volunteer work. First, volunteering helps you connect with other people. They say bending over to help someone up is the best exercise for the heart. Even doing small tasks can make you feel much happier. Volunteering also opens up the opportunity to make new contacts and friends.

When you volunteer it is an opportunity to increase your social skills and become more of a people person. Making connections with others and meeting new people are great ways to sharpen your social skills. Volunteering increases your self-confidence, helps depression and gives you a sense of purpose. Here are some ways to begin volunteering:

- Help out at the local school: Organize a drive to raise money to help out kids in need so that they can get materials that they need to complete the school year. Organize school supply drives at the library, or outside of office supply stores and grocery stores so that people can go in and buy supplies and drop them off with you on their way out.

    Recruit children to volunteer with you. Get more manpower to add to your volunteering efforts and teach children the value of volunteering by having them complete volunteer activities that are accessible to them, like organizing cans to donate to a food drive.

    Take children to a nursing home so that they can brighten the day of seniors. They can entertain residents that haven't received many visitors, and cheer them up. The children will learn to respect their older community members in the process.

- Help out from home: You can use your home to help others in need, like using it as a home base to produce crafts that can be sold for money to donate or handed out to seniors to brighten up their living areas.

    You can use your home as a center to cook meals for people in need. Meals are a great way to feed those who cannot afford to feed themselves, or families in need of services, such as military families.

- If you are an animal lover, do good deeds for your favorite furry friends. Local animal shelters always need more volunteers.

    If you have older neighbors or neighbors who are sick, offer to walk their dogs.

Consider putting together adoption kits that can be sent home with those who want to adopt pets from animal shelters.

- Reach out to military families. Cook meals for families who have had a member leave to serve the country, or buy these families groceries that they need.

Often times when we are on vacation we are more relaxed and friendly, therefore, it is in our nature to be kind to others. We'll hold the door open for someone or offer to help someone in need. Giving is rewarding and vacations are a mindset. Are you beginning to understand? You, my friend, are on vacation right now. Relax, be in the present moment. Enjoy this time. It is truly a vacation, and once you start to understand this, your entire body and soul will start to reap the benefits.

SAGE WILCOX

"I can't picture going to a beach, or anywhere on vacation, without a couple of books as companions."
~ Rosecrans Baldwin

12
TAKE A MINI VACATION – WITH YOURSELF!

The thought of being alone makes many of us uncomfortable. The journal *Science* suggested that people would rather give themselves electric shocks than be alone with their thoughts for more than fifteen minutes.

Some of us are introverts, about fifty percent of the population. This is perfectly OK! Although we are inundated with messages that it is extremely important to have a huge network of friends, to work in teams, and to be the center of attention, some people simply do not feel this way. For introverts, being in "social mode" can be fun, but it doesn't give them the most satisfaction or value from of their lives.

On the other side of the coin, extroverts get the most value and satisfaction from being in social mode and often like being the center of attention, but they can also have fun being by themselves. Being alone doesn't have to mean being lonely.

When you spend time alone and enjoy it, you feel more content about yourself. It also allows you to be introspective and get to know yourself better. Additionally, being alone can be a great opportunity to think about your issues and the best way to approach them.

You can take this time of being alone as a way to consider the possibilities you have in life. Planning the things, you would like to do in your life helps you to break your goals into smaller steps that are easier to attain.

Pressure to entertain someone, or to do things a certain way is not an issue when you are alone. You can see how spending time alone can reduce stress and help increase your feelings of relaxation. Here are some ideas on how to spend time alone:

How to Immerse Yourself in Soothing Solitude

Take the time to learn to be an observer out in public on your own. This entails looking at ordinary situations in new ways that are unfamiliar to you. Make a sincere effort to understand the people around you. When you learn about people around you, it helps you have more compassion and makes you feel connected to others.

Close your eyes in a darkened room and begin to appreciate the silence. Listen to everything that is happening around you, as well as everything that is not happening around you. When you do this you will learn the most about yourself.

Learn how to really talk to yourself. Every person has their own inner voice that speaks to them all of the time. Some say this inner voice is connected to God, some call it the Divine Source, some call it the Creator. Whatever you call it, getting to know and trust this inner voice, and how to productively listen to and communicate with it is one of the most important things you can do for yourself. Rather than asking others for advice, ask your inner self. And be kind to yourself. When you are on your own, take the time to distance yourself from the side of you that is negative and unproductive.

Where to Start

Being on your own has the potential to be scary. Think of it as a pool of cold water and just dive in. We all know that lowering ourselves into cold water feels uncomfortable at first, but eventually, it always turns out to be tremendous fun. And usually, in the end, we are so thankful that we took the plunge.

Start with a hobby to become familiar with solitude. Habits and hobbies that spark your imagination, consume your attention and inspire your creativity are the best activities to try on your own.

When you first begin to enjoy a mini vacation, change the environment. A change of scenery, like a new museum you have never been to can be a good way to edge into being comfortable by yourself.

Things to Do on Your Own

-Do not be afraid to go out by yourself. It can really boost your self-confidence and help you to feel more comfortable in your own skin, whether you go to the movies or out to eat on your own.

-Take time alone to enjoy a good book. Reading is not something you can really do with other people, anyway. Take advantage of being alone and immerse yourself in a good book that you can read every other day. It's a great way to shut your brain down and access the vacation mindset.

Here are some genres you might enjoy reading:

Read the Classics. These are the books you may have read

in high school, like "A Christmas Carol," "Moby Dick," or "Romeo and Juliet."

Explore Science Fiction. Some good places to start might be "Fahrenheit 451," or "I Robot."

Read Horror Novels. Try Steven King, or "Dracula."

Inhale Fantasy Fiction. "Lord of the Rings" or "Harry Potter" are popular titles in this genre.

General Fiction for Reading - "To Kill a Mockingbird" is a revered classic, as well as "Watership Down."

Read Some Poetry. Try Shakespeare's sonnets, or the works of Pablo Neruda.

Look at Plays. Some of the best playwrights are Neil Simon and Tennessee Williams.

-Take your time alone to explore new music or listen to your favorite songs. Often, being with other people prevents you from really listening to music.

-Try singing and dancing by yourself. You do not have to feel self-conscious because you are on your own. Let loose and have fun.

-Think about you. What do you believe in? Why? What things don't seem right to you, and what do you accept as a matter of faith? Start a journal and include this important information about yourself. Journaling is a form of healing and relaxation all on its own.

Vacation is a mindset. If you're not working, then you are on a vacation. It took a lot of practice for me to really get this and comprehend it, but once I did it became fun and enjoyable. And after a little while, my body totally relaxed into the idea. My mind, body, and soul loves being on vacation. Now, after I put a load of laundry in the washing machine, I know I have about an hour of "vacation" time. So what would I be doing if I were actually on a real vacation? For me it might be a nap, a bath, or reading. Vacation is a mindset, and my mind loves it!

SAGE WILCOX

"I envy people who can just look at a sunset. There is nothing more grotesque to me than a vacation."
~ Dustin Hoffman

13
SPEND A MINI VACATION WITH YOUR INNER CHILD

Sometimes one of the best ways to get away from it all is by channeling your inner child. Getting in touch with the child inside of us reminds us of a time when we were a blank slate – we felt wonder at the world around us in every way.

Channeling your inner child has many benefits that can help you in your adult life. When we were children, the adults around us often were telling us how to grow up, and this wasn't necessarily the best advice. Some of our most precious personal attributes come from when we were children. Here are some traits we had as kids that can help us to become an even more amazing adult:

- As children we were stubborn, courageous in the face of adversity: Children are resilient and stick to their beliefs no matter what. In adulthood, this can help us in our professional lives. The founders of Google were shot down numerous times before they got the company off of the ground, but they stuck to their guns. They didn't give up.

- Children questioned authority in a positive way: Children hate the phrases "because I said so", "Just because" or "because that's just the way things are done." They naturally challenge the status quo and embrace new ideas.

- Children are not afraid to pursue their passions: Once they set their minds to something, children won't stop until they get whatever it is they want to have or accomplish.

- Children indulge their egos when it works: Sometimes adults need to indulge their ego, like when we need to motivate or inspire our peers or coworkers.

- Children are natural risk takers: Children aren't afraid to make mistakes. Children aren't afraid of failure, and failure can be one of the most powerful tools for learning at any age. As adults, we don't like to make mistakes and often times feel like a failure when we do, instead of chalking it up to the learning lesson that it is.

- Children are great storytellers: It is easy for children to access their emotions and they tend to have little to no inhibitions. In our personal lives as adults, we form close connections with others who can easily access emotions and they remember the stories others share.

- Children often confront problems that arise head on. The childish tendency to be playing one second and to be at each other's throats, the next can actually be productive when adults channel this personality trait. If we as adults directly confront problems, rather than people, this can be harnessed for problem solving and professional success. It would be a benefit, as well, to forgive and forget as quickly as children do too.

- Finally, children can swallow their pride. As kids, we are taught to apologize when there is strife whether it is their fault or not. A sense of humor, as well as a sense of humility, are invaluable attributes for adults to have.

How to Channel Your Inner Child

Take inventory of the person you are today. What would your eight-year-old self think of you now? Would they be proud of the person you have become, your priorities and the decisions you have made?

Close your eyes and spend a few moments to think back to what it was like to be a young child. You were adventurous, silly, fun, fearless and loved simplicity. Open your eyes and jot down how you saw yourself as a child. What did you love about you when you were little? What were the things that made you happy? What was most important to you as a kid?

Imagine if you could reinvent yourself and become more like your eight-year-old self. Choose three adjectives that would best describe you as a child. In the following activities, make it a priority to become these words again. Drop your guard, trust your intuition and feel safe with the people around you.

Activities You Can Do to Channel Your Inner Child

What did you like to do as a child? What did like you watch? What did you read? What brought you joy? What was your favorite game? What was your favorite toy? Who were your heroes and why? What would you like to do with your inner child?

-Buy yourself a balloon

- Watch your old favorite cartoons on YouTube or Netflix, like the Sesame Street YouTube channel

- Treat yourself to some candy, or even some chocolate milk

- Play with wooden blocks, chalk, or Legos

- Swing on the swings

- Take some time to color – there are many coloring books for adults!

- Put together toy train tracks and just play

- Spend some time on a paint by numbers project

- Engage in physical play. Kick a ball around, and pretend that you are a professional soccer player

- Take a ride on a mountain bike

- Do crafts and don't be afraid to make a mess

- Build a fort with pillows and blankets

- Don't be afraid to cuddle an animal

- Gaze at the clouds and see what the shapes look like

- Read the "Velveteen Rabbit," a childhood favorite that taught us that life can be full of love even when it is torn and tattered.

- Make a sand castle on the beach

- Fold paper airplanes

- Play with puppies or kittens

- Draw pictures and tell the story of what you are drawing

Vacation is a mindset, and children love to play. Children really don't care if they go on some wild and exotic vacation. Give them a playground or a sprinkler system and they will have a blast. We recently got a large trampoline, and let me tell you, my inner-child comes out every time I jump on that thing. A few times a week I find vacation time to jump! Just tonight, I said to my daughter, "Hey the dishes are done, so I'm on vacation for the next 30 minutes. Do you want to go jump on the trampoline with me?" We jumped and laughed and had a splendid time, and my mind, body, and spirit reaped the benefits.

SAGE WILCOX

"My life is scattered and busy. I think of my home as a resort. When I step through the door, I feel relaxed. I feel like I've taken a vacation."
~ Chip Conley

Section Two

When we think of taking a break, the notion of taking a vacation is what springs to mind. Taking a vacation can be about seeing new sights, shopping, or even just getting pampered by first class hotel accommodation. They are all satisfying, albeit temporary surrogates for what you really need - which is to recharge your batteries and boost that diminishing vitality. There are three things of note that you should take into account on this.

First, notice how your mind wakes up and becomes more acutely aware of its surroundings after Wednesday moves into the rear-view mirror. That's because the body is motivated to get to the respite it longs for on the weekend. At the mere prospect of the weekend, the enthused mind leans towards the positive and that alters perceptions accordingly. Perceptions are everything. With a change in perception, reactions to external stimuli are altered, positively. They may not be huge changes, but they are cumulative.

Second, you seem to have a little more energy on Friday evening, even though you can feel the fatigue. It's not just the enthused mind, you also have an energized body. You feel the last ounces of energy mustered at the prospect of an anticipated event. There is an inherent expectation of downtime and the fond thoughts of waking up late or just catching up on reading while you doze off for a lazy afternoon nap. Your body and your spirit are piqued by this prospect of rest and the suspension of regular toil.

Third, there is the anticipation that you will come back to your natural clock. This, among the three reasons, is the most important reason for a vacation. The resetting of your rhythm and the rejuvenation of your vitality are two sides of the same coin of existence. The vacation that you seek is a vacation from the noise of chaos.

Reality

In the chapters that follow you will get an understanding that the mind sees only a version of reality. The mind is the sixth sense (not meant in the traditional sense meaning that it has extra sensory powers) that ties the data from the other five senses together and interprets the composite with logic that is unique to each individual. What it sees is your reality.

This is what we wish to alter - your reality. In fact, we want to suspend the data stream of your reality and transport you away from that data stream so that you are effectively on vacation from the things that usually stress you out. The reality that we want to alter is not designed to move you away from the truth, but closer towards it.

This is a virtual vacation. You don't need to imagine far away beaches, or exotic spas. Those fantasies might work for a moment, but you will find that your mind will quickly run out of realistic detail and the part of the mind that needs the vacation is no longer 'fooled' into thinking it's on one.

What you are going to do is get past the outward stimulation of a vacation that usually fill the commercial advertisement content, and look to the real effect and benefit of vacations - the silencing of the chaos. Once you silence the noise, the body will rejuvenate itself.

To silence the chaos, and look for the calm within, each day for just a few minutes will give you the effect of taking a mini vacation daily. It's inexpensive and it will not only boost your spirit, but also your body.

If you were on a vacation right now, what would you be doing? Let's get started.

1
I THINK THEREFORE I AM

"Cogito ergo sum" - I think, therefore I am. The infamous words penned by Rene Descartes carries varying degrees of meaning across the cerebral layers of our consciousness. Much of what happens around us is not really happening the way we think it's happening. Because what we think is happening, is exactly that - a thought, a notion, a comparison to something that we have experienced in the past.

It's not that we are living in a constant vegetative or delusional state. But if you reflect on it, the discussion of conscious awareness is highly subjective. There is a wide body of research and an even wider sea of opinion and conjecture about the mind and its ways.

What we have, when it comes to the study of the brain, is just inferences we can make by studying wide sample selections across statistically relevant swaths of society. But the one thing that is logical reality is that the key to everything that happens to us is not external to our being, it is internal and it is the engine that generates our perception when faced with any stimuli.

That engine, which is sometimes called a mindset, is tasked with pulling up the most relevant experiences and combining it with our philosophies. It also combines that with the current mood we are in. If you are in a lousy mood, chances are you're going to have a bad day. The reverse is also true.

If we start off with a predisposition towards the negative, then that's what our mindset is going to be. No matter what occurs externally after that, it will be perceived negatively. The topic of this book is not based on the reason the mind sees things through the lens of its present disposition, but instead, it is based on how the mind can create its own reality.

It means that you have control over what you see, believe, feel and experience regardless of what is going on around you. You literally have the power to shape the world around you. You can take anything that is thrown at you and mold it to your frame of mind. That power can build you up or break you down, the choice is yours. This book will show you how you can use it to rejuvenate, but really, there is no end to the possibilities that you have the power within to bring about. If you practice this (practice makes perfect, remember) you will have the ability to create anything that you desire.

You have to understand that anything you do can be broken down into three parts, or segments. The first is what happens - an event. The event can be internal or external, it can be real (as witnessed by more than one person) or it can be imagined (as witnessed by only you).

The second is the sensory perception of the event. For instance, if you stood facing the east on the beach when the sun begins to rise. Your visual senses (eyes) sees ever increasing light; your skin begins to feel the warmth of the rays. You can also feel the sand at the bottom of your feet and the rush of cool sea breeze. All of these are the sensations your body feels following an external event.

The third is the mind's processing of the event through the categorization, comparison, and storing of the event based on memory and logic.

Of the three steps, the third is the most critical. When you learn to control this part of your mind, you will be able to put yourself into any frame of mind at any time of the day. This is the part of the mind that Descartes talks about when he says, "I think, therefore I am". Because who you are is the event, what you feel are the sensory perceptions, and what your mind cogitates and determines is who you end up being in your own mind. And that last part is what you can determine. But like I stated above, when you learn to control this part of your mind, you will be in charge or your life and YOU will decide how you want it to be. Here's where the magic is. Here in step three. You are in control. You will learn how to tell you mind how it's going to be and how you are going to view things from here on out. No longer will your past situations, experiences, and observations randomly choose for you. This takes practice, but keep at it. It is worth it.

THE 2 – HOUR VACATION

"I don't wanna go on vacation. There's nothing about it that appeals to me. People look forward to doing that; I look forward to getting up every day and doing something."
~ Gene Simmons

2
HOW THE MIND WORKS

Your brain is not your mind. Your brain is the organ that sits in your cranial vault. It is made up of a number of distinct areas that control different parts of a person's overall presence, from mobility to personality, beliefs, and thoughts. Part of all the brain's responsibilities can occur beneath the radar of consciousness. For instance, it doesn't need conscious input to breathe, control heartbeat, balance hormones and so on.

Your mind on the other hand conceptually sits on top of your brain and is a framework consisting of ideas, notions, and memories, instead of being a physical object made of tissue. The mind cannot exist without the brain, but the brain does not need the mind as much. Although, a brain that doesn't get used (when the mind doesn't expand) has been known to regress physically and lose much of its capabilities.

We can think of our brain's scope of awareness as divided between internal and external perceptions of stimuli. Although our awareness is something we take for granted, it is the most important tool in our day to day interaction process. Our awareness juggles between pressures of external factors and demands of internal processes. There are two kinds of awareness we possess. The one that communicates with you, in a way that you can almost hear it, is the conscious awareness and the one that doesn't communicate with you, using language, is your subconscious awareness.

We are constantly left to manage between the external 'realities'; of our existence and circumstance, against the need to fulfill our internal purpose. From a biological perspective, our first and foremost objective is to survive and bear offspring to populate the next generation. The simple truth is that the human motivation is fairly simple, even if we go about achieving it in ever increasing complex ways. Our basic instincts are geared toward food, water, and procreation. Everything we do is ultimately purposed at achieving those three things.

Those basic instincts do not use spoken language to communicate with our conscious awareness. They do it in shades of feelings. Over time the mind begins to interpret those feelings and we respond appropriately. How well we interpret those sensations and feelings depends on a number of factors including how we were raised, the assumptions we make, the experiences that have been the result of those assumptions and a number of other circumstances.

Mindfulness

When you don't 'hear' something that is right next to you when you are fully concentrating on something else, it's not that your ears stop working. Instead, it is your brain that has stopped absorbing. In the midst of being busy, it has allocated all its conscious resources to the task at hand.

Your conscious mind has limited computing power (to

use a contemporary parlance) and only has the ability to process a limited set of stimuli or data. This is one of the reasons why when you have too much work to do and you have a lot on your mind, you get overwhelmed.

When the conscious mind gets overwhelmed by an abundance of data and stimuli, it kicks up a fuss. This is referred to as stress. Too much stress leads to mental fatigue. The threshold of stress and then fatigue is different for each person. Some people can take quite a bit before they stress out, others stress out at the slightest deviation from the ordinary.

It is this accumulation of stress and fatigue, otherwise referred to as stress (and the fatigue that ensues) that the vacation seeks to remedy.

The remedy is done by no effort on our part. It's like when you cut your finger. You just wash it, disinfect it, and the body will do the rest without you to interfere or administer. The same with the fatigue of the mind, body, and spirit. You just need to create the circumstances and let the body heal the mind.

Stress

Vacations are a three-dimensional proposition. They don't just change your surroundings and give you the opportunity to purchase tacky souvenirs from the gift shop. From the first time we take a vacation, probably as a kid dying to get away from the humdrum of school, we begin to appreciate the break in the monotony of stress.

Stress, whether we realize it, is an extremely insidious foe. It can zap out our will to fight, our strength to go on, and our clarity to focus. Stress takes a larger toll on our minds than it does on our bodies. This changes the way we view things around us, the things within us and the actions that ensue.

Stress increases intolerance and makes us combative (overtly and covertly). Stress is the reason we make errors in judgment, and it is the main reason our bodies have deteriorating immune systems.

It's a Turn On

The other reason we are turned on by vacations is that the mind is forced to wake up from its slumbering routine when the surrounding changes and the senses are heightened due to unfamiliarity. Having a nomadic streak since the time we took shape, our instincts wake up to the new environment and that invigorates our brain. The dopamine kicks in as a reward and all is fine with the world.

Now add the energized, dopamine filled brain, the diminished stress levels and the higher energy levels of a new surrounding, and what you have that has heightened your existence is all within you, not without. Your 'feel good' came from inside you. Granted it was sparked off by your surrounding. But even that surrounding is a mindset and the undeniable fact is that a mechanism in your body triggered the necessary responses to put you in a state of happiness, relaxation, and peace.

Vacations are meant to relax the mind and allow it time to purge the accumulated mental toxins that build up with disappointments, stress, fatigue and so on. Vacations have all the ingredients to heal and rejuvenate the mind because of the three factors mentioned earlier. Mindfulness exercises, meditation, and visualization are all the different techniques you can use to effect the same results in your mind. This virtual vacation works just as well and is more efficient at purging the mental toxins, thereby allowing your mind and body to heal faster.

*"I always tell my kids make your
vocation your vacation."
~ Chynna Phillips*

3
THE VACATIONING MIND

Your mind is designed to be the interface between you and the world around you. You can verify this fact by observing how people from different cultures respond to the same external stimuli. Some people eat bugs and find it healthy, others see bugs served for a meal and would turn green. The mind, more specifically the conscious mind, takes the sensory input data and makes sense of it based on teachings, experiences, habits, and then forms a deep memory of it.

Between the time it collects the data and interprets it for further action there is a temporal gap as well as a conceptual gap that gives rise to a number of bridging phenomena. Bridging phenomena are things like a person's mindset or tolerance. A person with a positive mindset will take any external stimuli and processes it with the means to a positive outcome. The person with a negative mindset will have a negative analysis and eventually a negative outcome.

This is the gap that some people condone injecting fantasy to simulate vacations. For instance, you could strap on a virtual reality device and feed your mind the information here.

When fantasy is injected here, the rest of the mind has no realization whether the stimuli is real (everyone can see it) or imagined (only you can see it). In this case, the mind takes it as real, as long as all the logical parameters are fulfilled.

One of the ways this works adversely is in patients with schizophrenia. They absolutely see, hear, smell, feel and thus believe they are in a different reality than they really are. This just goes to show the point; it's not meant to make a case of mimicking hallucinations as a substitute for vacations.

However, there are some strategies floating on the net where they ask you to fantasize about being on vacation. That is nowhere nearly the same thing as what this book is describing. In fact, fantasies and fantasizing are not as rewarding in the long run. In the short run, they do not address the issue of rejuvenation and returning peace to your soul. Fantasizing may seem appropriate but it will leave you disappointed at the end and that adds to the mental stress and fatigue.

Although fantasizing is a good start, long-term it can actually increase the stresses of your mind, because, subconsciously your mind knows that to a certain extent there is a glitch with the 'reality' that is in front of it. The real vacationing mind is given respite from its daily grind so that it can purge the toxins and rejuvenate itself. That's what we want to emulate and we will do that by following the simplest practice to make your mind believe from its deepest folds that it is time to rejuvenate.

The juxtaposition between the temporal gap and the conceptual gap is a void. A void only because we do not have the sensory mechanisms to detect it except through the feeling of silence. More on this later.

"I'm a big believer in living life as an extended working vacation."
~ Victoria Moran

4
YOU CAN DO THIS AT HOME

If you recall that the reason a vacation works so well is because the mind is shuttled away from the source of all its tensions and stress. Without additional stress, the body begins to recover and gets jazzed up for the next string of events. That's what vacation should do. To mimic, you need to give your mind and body the chance to recover and recuperate.

You can do this at home because this is really a mind hack and so there is no travel needed. These are what we call mini vacations.

Locate yourself in a part of your home where there is the least amount of distractions. None of your senses should be called to serve while you are in this state because that will disrupt the illusion.

You will first start with mindfulness exercises but remember these are not religious or spiritual in nature. They can be if you choose to, but in and of themselves they are not. When you close your eyes, do not pay attention to the visions that flash before you in your mind's eye, but rather locate the sound that your breathing makes.

Once you locate that sound, as subtle as it may be, affix your attention to that gentle rhythm. Do not try to alter your breathing or change the volume of the sound it makes. Leave your breath the way it was before you went in search of it. If your breath is so silent that you can't detect it, then observe the heaving of your chest as your diaphragm expands and contracts.

From there, transition to the movement of the breath in and out of your nostrils. There will be distractions from within. That's natural. Your mind was designed to fill your conscious moments with a voice. In fact, it does the same when you are asleep, that's what we call dreams. The brain does not shut down and it will always throw up thoughts. It's ok, it's not broken. But to kick off a mini vacation, it's time to turn away from those thoughts and voices.

Focusing on your breath is the best way to get started because the natural rhythm breathing has the ability to pull your focus away from almost anything you need it to. Once you have your sites trained firmly on your breathing, you will begin to feel like a body of water that is chaotic and left to rest as it slowly calms itself to complete stillness.

Once you have followed your breath to this point. It is time to go to the next waypoint. Here your guiding beacon is silence. Just as you listened for the silence of your breath and felt the undulating motions of your chest, now you go in search for the silence that is deepest inside you. Again, this is not of a religious nature, but in many religions of the world, silence is something that is revered, and also sometimes misunderstood. In most houses of worship, especially Christian ones, the sanctity of the House of God is marked by reverent silence. In fact, you are asked to pray in silence.

The Importance of Silence

When you are asked to pray in silence, it is not just the volume of the surrounding area that is being described. It is that, but it is a lot more. In addition to finding solace in a silence, you are being asked to pray in the language of silence.

Silence is not the absence of sound, just as courage is not the absence of fear. Silence is the language of the universe and it is the core of our being. When we pray in silence, it just means that we are not mumbling words, but we are letting the silence in the core of our soul communicate with eternity.

When you find this silence, and you are in its presence nothing else around you can disturb or shake the peace. Here you are opened to the vastness of all existence. Here you become one with creation.

Silence is the key. Before the big bang, before the creation of light, before everything, there was silence. It is the very nature that pervades us at the deepest level. When you reach this state of silence, your body, brain, mind all go into automatic rejuvenation mode.

The Lack of Stimulation

Inside that silence, there is a lack of any form of stimulation. You are oblivious to the distractions outside and you don't pay any attention to any of the thoughts or memories that your brain is kicking up. By the way, while you are in this state, your brain is still creating thoughts and bringing up old memories. You just can't see them because you have chosen the silence.

This lack of stimulation gives your body and mind a moment to rest and get away from the stresses of your daily routine.

Those who practice this level of mindfulness and silent prayer report that they feel 100% rejuvenated when they return to the world around their physical bodies. There are three things you can anticipate after just 15 minutes of silent meditation.

First, upon returning to your physical location, you will feel a sense of vitality that you didn't have when you began the exercise. If it doesn't happen the first day, do not be alarmed. It takes a few days and practice for you to get used to the transition from sensory overload to focusing on just your breathing and transition onwards to embracing the silence.

Second, you will find that you have a little more energy than you had before you entered the state of silence. This energy is not a figment of your imagination. The energy moves from inside you and all around you. There is enough energy in you at any given point in time to allow you to fast for more than 2 - 4 weeks. With that kind of energy, it's unimaginable to those who practice silence that you could ever run out in the middle of the day. This is not the loss of energy but the sensation of fatigue. When you feel the added sense of energy, what is really going on is that you are no longer fatigued from the accumulation of stress.

The third aspect of the silent meditation is that you return to your natural time. One of the best ways to rejuvenate yourself is to slow your time down. Slowing your time can happen in one of two ways, you can either travel at really fast speeds (Einstein's Relativity) and that slows your time down or you can return to silence and your natural rhythm through the silent meditation.

The second way is preferable. When our parents told us that silence is golden, we had no idea how true that statement really is.

"If we would only give, just once, the same amount of reflection to what we want to get out of life that we give to the question of what to do with a two weeks' vacation, we would be startled at our false standards and the aimless procession of our busy days."
~ Dorothy Canfield Fisher

5
THE RHYTHM OF SILENCE

By taking these short vacations every day for a few minutes at a time, we attain the level of rejuvenation we need. Some practitioners can do with 20 minutes of silent meditation what a normal person can do with a three days' worth of regular sleep. These journeys to silence can put you back in touch with a source that is awakened and it stirs the same in you.

There are no religious connotations to any of this and you should continue your practice of worship without interruption. These silent meditations are not a part of any religion or religious practices. It is as religious as taking a nap.

Take all of this slowly. Try not to cram it in a day. Also do it consistently. Do it every day. And within a few days, what you will find is that your new found energy makes you effective.

Do not take becoming super effective lightly, we need to let the experiences of the mind sink in. Imagine pouring water on a dry bed of soil. If you pour too much, the patch floods and eventually the water above ground evaporates, doing no good to the soil. On the other hand, if you spread a little first, allowing it to break the arid soil and sink in, then add a little more, then a little more, each time punctuating the act with a period of rest, the soil and your crop will benefit more.

If directly translated it seems like the best way to get through life is to take vacations daily, or something of similarly balanced work to rest ratio.

But before that, we must also realize that the body and mind are designed to work. When we rest too much, our muscles atrophy, our mind turns to mush and our spirit is lost roaming the corridors of vacant space. When we work, we end up being productive, when we are productive we contribute, when we contribute, our existence matters.

The perfect balance is struck when you work and strive to contribute and participate in society and build your life around that and your family. The demands of your place in society is counterbalanced by your return to silence daily - your daily vacation - in an effort to rejuvenate and fortify the wears of the day. Whatever toxins that build up in the framework of your mind is flushed out, whatever has eroded is rebuilt and whatever is needed is found.

CONCLUSION

Wherever we are, whatever we do, the one thing that stays the same is us. We are the one element in the equation that remains constant. Whether it is being in Havana, and absorbing the waves of the Caribbean dancing to the throbbing Rumba, or in your backyard swaying in a hammock listening to the birds sing their sweet melody. It doesn't matter where you are, you are the one thing that never changes in the picture in that moment in time.

Moving one step deeper, you realize that not only are you the only thing that doesn't change, but (as mentioned earlier) you also have the power to change the reality that's around you.

How can this be right? It's right because you shape your reality. If you believe that getting sick after rain is true, it will happen to you. Your reality is shaped by you. Now imagine turning this same mechanism around to work for you. And you can do it. Turn this around so that you can make whatever you want to be true in life happen for you.

It all comes down to our individual mindset, what we believe and how we perceive. The best way to fortify your mindset is to also practice your silent meditation. As innocuous as it may seem to sit still in silence, this silent stillness is one of the most effective ways to chip away at mistaken perceptions and expectations thereby reducing one of the long term stress inducers. We do not realize it but our expectations place a tremendous burden on us and that leads to stress.

Once we handle our perceptions, and our mindsets are attended to, stresses are better handled. It is our mindset that advances ahead of our physical self to create an expectation of an impending event. It is our mindset that paints a picture of a vacation, full of freedom, lack of deadlines and non-existent social pressures. All those expectations, countless numbers of associative images, and fantasies can paint a destination positively, as opposed to painting it with drudgery when it is for work. It's all in your mind. Once you get over the expectations, you will begin to see the truth in all things and realize that the best vacation is the one where you sit in the comfort of your home in total peace and return to your silence every day.

AFTERWORD

Explore these activities and tips to bring some simple joy into your life. Lower your inhibitions and don't be afraid to make mistakes. Experiment with the concepts that you find appealing and do more of what you enjoy the most. These ideas are just the tip of the iceberg. When you find something that works for you more ideas and activities will come.

We work hard, and we should treat ourselves with care because we all deserve peace and happiness. No matter who we are, we are all special and can take a mini vacation no matter how busy we are, no matter what our resources are, and no matter how much money we have.

When we are kind to ourselves, our work-life becomes more productive, our health is improved, and possibly the best thing is that our kindness will benefit the people around us, from strangers to the people we love the most.

Taking the time to read this book is your first step. As the book discussed it can be a little scary to jump into the cold water, but once you do; once you get used to the temperature, you will end up satisfied and fulfilled, therefore, reap the benefits. Do not be afraid to treat yourself to a mini vacation. Just a few hours a week can improve your life dramatically.

WHAT WE DO

We are often asked what we do for 2-hour vacations. Once we learned how to practice this, it became fun and easy. We have trained our minds to recognize that if we are not working, then we are indeed on vacation. Making this simple change – changing the way we think - changed everything. We changed our belief system. We formed a new way of thinking and this new way of thinking became a habit. As time went on, our family and friends noticed a positive difference in us. We were happier and healthier. We were relaxed and calm at family gatherings. People started asking us what we were doing different. So we started telling them, and many could relate and once we explained the concept they really got it. Others started making the changes and before we knew it they started contacting us to tell us how wonderful their lives were becoming because of it. As I mentioned earlier, we taught our children to have a vacation mindset as well. When we get a break from the mundane household chores and tasks, we tell our kids that we have a certain amount of "vacation time" available, and then we have fun being on vacation!

The other thing we discovered is that "real" vacations are overrated. Our mother-in-law recently rented a camp on the ocean for one week. She paid $2500 and by the end of the week, she couldn't wait to get home. She even thought about going home early. She spent two days packing before the trip, one day packing up at the end of her vacation, and three days unpacking once she got home. Two weeks later our sister-in-law and her family rented a camp on a nearby lake. She couldn't wait to get home either. As a matter of fact, a couple days that week she did go home (it was only a 40-minute drive), and still by the end of the week, she couldn't wait to get home. Although my in-laws had some fun during their week vacations, they were tired, spent a lot of money, and couldn't wait to get back to the comforts of their own homes.

Here are some of the things that we do on a regular basis to rejuvenate our minds, bodies, and souls:

We play cards and board games often. (That's what we'd do if we were on vacation!)

Have a picnic.

Go to the beach.

Take a nap.

Read a good book

Tent out in the backyard.

Take a bath with low lighting/candles.

Play with our pets.

Meditate. – This is the key!

Have campfire nights where we make s'mores.

Popcorn and movie nights.

THE 2 – HOUR VACATION

Find new things to do locally.

Find new places to explore in our home state.

Go hiking.

Foot soak.

Snow-shoeing.

Drink hot chocolate by a warm fire.

Make and drink our favorite drinks.

Have dance parties in the living room.

Play ping-pong on our kitchen table.

Give each other massages.

Look up at the sky.

Watch the clouds and pick out images that we see.

Feed the ducks.

Bird watching.

Bike riding.

Walks.

Home manicures and pedicures.

Jump on our trampoline.

Paint and do crafts.

Simplify our home – we are striving to make our home be more like a camp. Simple and easy. We've found that the reason we can relax in a hotel room or at camp, is because there isn't much clutter in these places. We've found that clutter and "stuff" is exhausting to look at and be around.

We purchased an old boat for less than $1000. We use it as a floating camp. We rent a boat mooring less than a mile from our home and we take 2 hour vacations on our boat often. Most of the time we just leave it on the mooring. It's simple and easy and swimming around the boat and having picnics on it has been such a fun and relaxing experience.

***

So there you have it. Those are a few things that we do on a regular basis to relax. It's been amazing and freeing for us.

Remember vacation is a mind-set. You can be on vacation any time that you want and you should! Learn to enjoy your downtime, and teach your family how to enjoy their time as well. You'll be glad that you did!

If you have other ideas or want to share your success stories, please feel free to send me an email at: sagewilcoxbooks@gmail.com

I look forward to hearing from you! Thanks!

ABOUT SAGE WILCOX

Sage lives in the United States with her husband of 15 years, children, cat and dog. She is a certified energy healer and is working on becoming a Life Coach. Sage enjoys giving advice to her clients, friends, and family on healing, love and relationships. She also enjoys studying human behavior, reading, writing, being outdoors, and enhancing her relationships with others. She enjoys growing closer to the Divine Source and reading and learning the Bible and scripture. In her experience, the more she learns and practices the Word, the better her life becomes.

Sage is a hopeless romantic! She strives to help others fall madly in love with everything about their lives! That includes all things most people would consider boring. There's no room for boring in Sage's life. She likes to spice life up in every way!

Sage has also written:

> *Love Letters from Exes: Proof That Life Goes On After a Break Up and Love Is What You Make It*
>
> *Until We Fall*

Please visit her website at:

http://sagewilcox.wix.com/books

Disclaimer

The purpose of this book is for entertainment purposes only. This is a work of fiction and names, characters, businesses, places, and incidents are either the products of the authors' imaginations or used in a fictitious manner. Any resemblance to actual persons, living or dead, businesses, companies, events, locales, or actual events is entirely coincidental. The author and publisher are not engaged in rendering medical, psychological, legal, or any other professional services. If medical, psychological or other expert assistance is required, please talk to your physician and locate the services of a competent professional. The author and publisher shall have neither liability nor responsibility to any person or entity with respect to any loss or damage caused, or alleged to have been caused, directly or indirectly, by the information contained in this book. Neither the publisher nor the individual author(s) shall be liable for any physical, psychological, emotional, financial, or commercial damages, including, but not limited to, special, incidental, consequential or other damages. Our views and rights are the same: You are responsible for your own choices, actions, and results. If you do not wish to be bound by the above, you may return this book along with a copy of the receipt to the publisher for a full refund.

www.ingramcontent.com/pod-product-compliance
Lightning Source LLC
Chambersburg PA
CBHW070642050426
42451CB00008B/262